AF114429

PHILIP D. RYE

ALL SHAPES AND SIZES

ALL SHAPES AND SIZES

© 2024 Philip D. Rye

The right of Philip D. Rye to be identified as the author of this work has been asserted by him in accordance with the Copyright, Designs and Patents Act, 1988.

All Rights Reserved

No part of this book may be reproduced in any form by photocopying or by an electronic or mechanical means, including information storage or retrieval systems, without permission in writing from the copyright owner and author of this book© 2024 Philip D. Rye

Published by BoD · Books on Demand, Oslo, Norway
Printed by Libri Plureos GmbH, Friedensallee 273, 22763 Hamburg, Germany

ISBN: 978-82-845-1069-9

ALL SHAPES AND SIZES

 You don't need to read this bit, it is way less interesting than the rest of the book, but it might provide some context to how the stuff printed on the following pages came into being. *All Shapes and Sizes* is an eclectic blend of rhyming verse, illuminating the trivialities of everyday life and communication to more thought-provoking subjects such as the nature of loss. These have on many occasions evoked laughter and even tears. Yes, I really have made people cry with my poetry, which is no small achievement especially with a softback cover. Sources of inspiration have been many and varied, either through empathic projection, or personal experience. Often a simple remark or a facial expression has initiated the creative cascade. Many of my more creative moments have occurred while sitting on the toilet. For this I make no apology: Quality time alone with one's thoughts is not to be underestimated. The classic pose by Auguste Rodin's sculpture of The Thinker was no coincidence, although Rodin opted for discretion in his final sculpture: The absence of a porcelain throne to collect the by-products of his thinking time was simply an omission that ensured his work would have wider appeal to a more refined and cultured audience. I have taken a less discerning approach. That said, I believe more people should get back into the closet and discover the power of uninhibited and undisturbed thought. Anyway, enough of me flushing lyrical… be brave and read on. Much of the good stuff is in the middle, so just dip in and out, don't read it straight through or you will constipate your senses.

PDR 2024

Contents

All Shapes And Sizes	12
Au Revoir	13
Bad Hair Days	14
Bewildered	15
Breathing Space	16
Chemistry – Blind	17
Chemistry – Deaf	18
Chemistry – Dumb	19
Chocolate	20
Complicated Beasts	21
Complementary Forces	22
Conversations	23
Contranyms – I	24
Contranyms – II	25
Dementia – Mental Disconnection	26
Dementia – Recognition Denied	27
Dementia – Two Deaths	28
Dementia – Thanks For The Memory	29
Diamonds	30
Excuse Me Have We Met	31
Fantasies	32
Frequent Flyer	33
Growing Old – I	36
Growing Old – II	37
Growing Old – III	38
Honesty Or Truth	39
Hotel Guests	40
Hung-Over	41

Hung-Over Again	42
Inside Your Smile	43
In Your Own Hands	44
Judgement	45
Just One Kiss	46
Language	47
Late	48
Letting Go	49
Life Without Love	50
Meaning Less	51
Memories	52
Mirror Mirror	53
Miss Communication	54
More or Less	55
Mosquito Nights	56
Motel Blues	58
My Brother	59
No Body's Perfect	60
Not All Wounds Bleed	61
Not So Nursery Rhyme – Humpty	62
Not So Nursery Rhyme – Mary	63
Not So Nursery Rhyme – Muffet	64
Not So Nursery Rhyme – Owl	65
Not So Nursery Rhyme – Sheep	66
Not So Nursery Rhyme – York	67
Pandemic	68
Parallel Uni-Verse	69
Pissing In The Wind	70
Politicians And Prostitutes	71
Pubic Hairs	72
Sheets	73

Signal Failure	75
Size Is Everything	76
Speechless	77
Team Player	78
The Soul	79
That Kind Of Girl	80
The Backside Of Your Smile	81
The Beautiful Chest	82
The Big C	84
The Royal Throne	85
Thinking About Thinking	86
Tongue In Cheek	87
Travel Tip	88
Undertakers	89
Valentine	90
Vital Organs	91
Warm Seats	92
Wedding Night	93
When I Lay Down	95
When Things Go Wrong	96
Wisdom	97
Xposure	98

All Shapes And Sizes

The one thing that shines
Through all manner of disguises
Is that stupidity comes
In all shapes and sizes.

Au Revoir

As you turn your back to leave
The refrain drifts in the air
"Au revoir", "see you soon"
But do you really care?
Or is it just something that is said
On occasions such as these
A social punctuation mark
To make us feel at ease?
When what you really meant to say
As you raised your hand to wave
Was that you hope we never meet again
This side of the grave!

Bad Hair Days

I've heard it said, but never read
That every hair upon your head
Can, quite independent of your brain
Drive you totally insane
It's unbelievable to think
That these strands around the sink
While just a fraction of your total weight
Contribute to your mental state
But this they do with expertise
These temperamental devotees
Of quarrelsome quiffs and unwelcome waves
Are master architects of bad hair days.

Bewildered

You looked at me, but spoke no words
An ear could ever hear
Bewildered
You left me wondering
Your message wasn't clear
Enthralled
By what you might have said
(You're oblivious to my plight)
I thought I 'heard' you
Loud and clear, but
Did I get the message right?

Breathing Space

One day
This will be ten years away
Your tears
A jaded memory
Your fears
Abandoned in the rush of hope
Your pain
Just history
But now
No cliché
Can replace
The need for silence
And a breathing space.

Chemistry – Blind

I feel you near
I know you're here
I cannot see your face
But chemistry, with no eyes to see
Only requires a place.

Chemistry – Deaf

The chemistry that we once had
Has now reached a steady state
A social equilibrium
A relationship stalemate
I am blind to your advances
I am deaf to your appeals
And cannot seem to find the words
To tell you how I feel
So what future lies ahead?
What elements can I add
To the chemical reaction
That once drove us both so mad?
Maybe you'll be smart enough
Devise a new formulation
So when I'm done being blind, deaf and dumb
It will improve our communication.

Chemistry – Dumb

When you're here I cannot speak
You disrupt all I plan to say
The ordered, clear and lucid thoughts
Temporarily thrown in disarray
The same for you, I see is clear
What senses have we stirred?
This chemistry, so tangible
The equilibrium
Disturbed.

Chocolate

You have captivated millions
You have melted on their lips
You have prostituted purity
To retain them in your grip
Yet without criminal intent
Your sole purpose is to please
The populations of the world
With satisfying ease.

Complicated Beasts

True love complicates desire
They are independent beasts
That should be locked in cages
With different sets of keys.

Complementary Forces

There's no froth without fizz
No Taylor without Liz
No flame without fire
No passion, desire
Flesh without bone
House, home
Death, life
Husband, wife
No Yang without Yin
No religion without sin
No guilt without wrong
No singers no song
Love without strings
Engagement, rings
No was without is
No froth... no fizz.

Conversations

I love our conversations
Your intellect astounds
Your knowledge
Is overwhelming
Your insight knows no bounds
But all these conversations
Only serve to fill-in time
When really, I'd rather synchronize
Your lips
And mine.

Contranyms – I

The English language seems designed to confuse
With silent H's and superfluous U's
Aside from odd rules, which are just anti-social
We have thousands of words at our disposal
So, with all these words
Why on earth do we bother
To make one word have two meanings
That are the reverse of each-other?

Contranyms – II

Clip:
A clip is a cut to separate or dissect
Unless it's a clip used to bind or connect.

Dust:
To add a powder to something or wipe it away
Means I can dust and get nowhere all bloody day.

Fast:
Fast can mean really quick, if you're in luck
Otherwise, it's the opposite, and you're stuck.

Stroke:
A stroke is a sign of tender affection
But can also be a terrible neurological affliction.

Transparent:
To be transparent is obvious to you and me
Unless it is something that no one can see.

Variety:
A variety can be one of any
Unless one implies a selection of many.

Dementia – Mental Disconnection

With each step you take
In your mental disconnection
I lose you by degrees
With your endless repetition

In your endless repetition
I am driven to despair
But this is your dementia
And you are blissfully unaware

That you are blissfully unaware
Is a merciful exception
In this unforgiving spiral
Of losing your perception

But while this lost perception
Means nothing more to you
This mental disconnection
It is my dementia too.

Dementia – Recognition Denied

He sat
She watched
He smiled
She cried
Alas recognition
Denied
Where is the one
She loved?
Still loves?
Is he in there?
Has he gone?
What evil
Isolates the mind
And leaves
This empty shell
Behind?

Dementia – Two Deaths

Radical theories in Alzheimer's
Suggest there's a critical cascade
Of events that once set in motion
Are impossible for us to evade
Proteins conspire to evict us
Disrupt what we think we control
Our thoughts, our memories, our identity
Squeezed like a sponge from the soul
Yet the body continues to function
Long after our memories have left
I know I must soon die of something
But I'd rather die only one death.

Dementia – Thanks For The Memory

My short-term memory has shortened
My hippocampus shrunk
So cognitively impaired that
I might as well be drunk
My p-tau's have helped to tie the knot
Determining the fate
Of all my little neurons
Failure to communicate
My vacuoles are vacant
White matter's going 'West'
Assaulted by amnesia
I am failing every test
So I get no silver plated trophy
Just simple little plaques
An amyloid reminder
Of my amnestic attacks
Maybe my pathologist
Has the appropriate technology
To have these little plaques engraved
With, "Thanks for the Memory".

Diamonds

So, he said to her
"Let me show you diamonds like you've never seen
With beauty unsurpassed by fabricated jewellery"
He took her hand
And led her through the busy streets
Over pavements
Crossing roads
Past expensive boutiques
And there
Towards the edge of town
He pointed up
"Oh wondrous sight!"
She followed his direction
And stared into the winter's night
A gasp? Surprise?
A time for romantic thoughts to linger?
She gazed once more upon their natural beauty and replied
"But I want one on my finger!"

Excuse Me Have We Met

She smiled at me, so I smiled too
I politely said "hello"
But she mistook the gesture
As if I was someone she should know
Perhaps it was the tone of voice
Or my uncertain glance
Implying that we'd met before
This awkward circumstance.

Fantasies

There is a place I feign control
Where untold piles of luggage lie
In a labyrinth of rusty lockers
Invisible to the naked eye
There, the strangest contents of my mind
Disquiet the essence of my soul
And questions the very reason
Why this place exists at all.

All these fantasies I hide
In the corners of my head
Where many untold dreams persist
Often better left unsaid
But should they disappear
As one day I know they could
Would my sanity evaporate?
Regrettably, I fear it would.

Frequent Flyer

Long haul
Short haul
Life's a ball
If you're a frequent flyer.

Constant noise
Feeling harassed
Intimate with strangers
Of unknown past
Sharing their odours
And their diseases
Second-hand air
Full of coughs and sneezes.

Fat folk, dull folk
Drunk and rude
I'm a grumpy passenger
If I don't get my food
Wherever I sit
I get the meal trolley last
Five minutes to landing
So I have to eat fast.

In flight magazines
Duty free sale
Perfume and chocolates
Airlines regale
In flight movies
Seen them before

I try to watch but
It's such a bore.

Loyalty programs
Bonus miles
Host and hostesses
Force feed smiles
Queues for the loo
Where you can't swing a cat
Pee on my shoe
I should have sat.

Turbulence
Flatulence
Try to suppress it
Spent too long in this seat
Now I can't feel my feet
Oh god what a prognosis
When all this ends, I'll get
Deep vein thrombosis.

Screaming child
I shouldn't complain
Parents can't help it
But they're the ones I blame
Pressure has built up
Their ears can't pop
I try to feel pity
But the screams won't stop

Is there a remote possibility
To get me home quickly

To speed up this journey
To some peace and tranquility?
Just get me out of this tube
And home to my wife
So I can stop frequent flying
And get on with my life.

Growing Old – I

Youth once reigned taut about the eyes
Now slack with bags and laughter lines
While sagging cheek and folded jowls
No blade or potion can cajole
Thus
However earnest
However rich
Gravity will always win
That heartless bitch.

Growing Old – II

Fear not gentle father time
Accept his relentless way
Your face will get fewer wrinkles
And your hair, less grey
But, have more respect
For the depravity
Exercised by his evil relative
Gravity.

Growing Old – III

When the tits go south
It's a bummer
But at least the wee birds come back north
For the summer.

Honesty Or Truth

Truth is a double edge sword
And is a powerful thing
Even if you're the one waving it around
Look out for the backswing.

Hotel Guests

The bed was made
The bathroom cleaned
But still there was a trace
Within this room
A memory left
In molecules of the air
We shared
Not time
Only this space.

Hung-Over

The big white telephone was ringing
I had to take the call
Although my head was spinning
From too much alcohol.

It was Uncle Huey
With a belated reminder
From him and auntie Spewy
About not going on a blinder.

Although it had been a while
Since our last communication
I recalled the evil taste of bile
As I began our conversation!

Hung-Over Again

My head spins through a familiar refrain
As I bend to greet the porcelain
To cast an offering in the bowl
In penance for my lost control.

Inside Your Smile

I want to step inside your smile
Enjoy its warm embrace
Cleanse the palate of my mind
My anxious thoughts replace
With a treasure island dream
Where crystal-coloured seas
Meet foaming sands of white champagne
Stirred by a gentle breeze
And while the rhythm of the waves
Breathes up and down that shore
I am refreshed inside your smile
But wish that you would smile more.

In Your Own Hands

What is fortune?
What is fate?
Our lives are simply
What we create
The cards are dealt
We have no say
In what we're given
Only how we play.

Judgement

Never judge a person
By their hair, clothes or colour
Always by their smile, their eyes
And of course, their sense of humour.

Just One Kiss

If I could only snatch the chance
Or happen on a circumstance
Wherein our lips would simply meet
Like passing friends along the street
What would you do, what would you say?
Would you instinctively pull away
Or linger there without restrain
Until the need to breathe again?
Then I could wish for time to stop
While our sweet dancing lips would not
But what cruel fantasy is this?
All I ask is just a kiss.

Language

Italians shout too much
The French, slur their speech
The English lips are far too stiff
And difficult to teach
The Germans are too guttural
A harsh and throaty touch
Just like the Arabs, Finns and Latvians
And, of course, the Dutch
While Nordic lands have melody
Some pleasing to the ear
But it's hard to shape the mouth
To make the sounds they need to hear
While those in Spain
Set a cracking pace
Through every single syllable
As if speaking was a race
Similarly, as if to save on time
The Danes cut short and thin
Abbreviating whole sentences
So they can fit more in
But what about the body?
A language world renowned
A communication medium
Without uttering a sound
We underestimate its value
And ability to display
Since what we do means so much more
Than anything we say!

Late

I'm always late, you know it's true
But is it such a crime?
Since, if you know I'm always late
Then actually I'm on time!

Letting Go

Just lately, I feel
You do not feel the same
That somehow, with each passing day
Your thoughts for me have passed away
Replaced
Behind once radiant eyes
A distance, your smile cannot disguise.

Am I too late
Too old, too slow
To change the way you feel for me?
Too blind, or just too dumb to see
That this
Subtle ebb of feelings show
It's just your way of letting go.

Life Without Love

A life without love
Is a car without wheels
It's a book with no story
A restaurant with no meals
It's a forest without trees
It's a chair with no seat
It's a petting zoo without pets
It's a cavalry charge in retreat
It's a house with no roof
No floors and no walls
A life without love
Is no life at all.

Meaning Less

Love is a word
Whose meaning was lost
While being tossed
From meaning to meaning.
Over-use it
And you lose its force
Force someone to say it
And you lose its meaning.

Memories

Time has no memory
But memories own time
Hours own minutes
But all the minutiae are mine.

Mirror Mirror

Mirror, mirror on the wall
Who's the most beautiful of all?
Surely you know me well enough to say
That I'm the best you've seen today?

"Well, I cannot lie you are the best
But then, I haven't really seen the rest."

Mirror, mirror, please be kind
It's getting easier to find
These lines that crease upon my brow
Tell me who is the prettiest now?

"Well since it's you, I'll be discrete
That lipstick does look rather cheap."

Mirror, mirror, tell me true
You know I've never lied to you
Please do tell me to my face
Is everything in its proper place?

"Each time we meet, you always whine
Which has not eased with passing time
It's honesty you seek, so I confess
You've always looked a dreadful mess!"

Miss Communication

She thought she heard the words he thought
She read meanings that were never meant
She said
He thought
But neither heard
And so their conversations went.

More or Less

All these troubling secrets
That I choose to keep suppressed
What damage would they cause
Should they ever be confessed?
Would they bring us closer
Or would they bring me shame?
Would you love me more or less
Or more or less the same?

Mosquito Nights

Lying in a stuffy room
Beads of sweat appear
The unyielding humid summer's night
Typical for the time of year
Window wide, body bare
You linger on the verge
Dreamily, not quite here
Nor there... then suddenly a power surge!

Your whole body, tense for action
To a sound you've always feared
You sit up wide-eyed, wide-awake
But, it has mysteriously disappeared
As minutes pass you see no point
Staring round the airless room
So reluctantly you settle down
Knowing that it will resume.

Then suddenly it's there again!
Whining in your ear
Your arms urgently lash out
At everything that's near
Wild eyed, like a lunatic
You try to find the source
Of this night's anxiety, unaware
The sound has changed its course.

Then, moments later upon the wall
Disproportionate in size

To the terror it inflicts upon you
A tiny... little... fly
You raise your hand and slapping hard
Triumphantly to show
A mangled exoskeleton
But alas, you were too slow.

Meanwhile your heart is pounding
The drumming inside your head
Drives out all possibility of sleep
As you settle back upon the bed
Where fate decides, enough's enough
The competition is too quick
And the evil monster seals its doom
With a thirsty little prick.

Then suddenly a reflex!
Spontaneous at this time of night
Moves your flattened hand
Through the air (at about the speed of light)
This movement finally strikes the blow
That secures the creature's doom
And returns a welcome silence
To your hot and sweaty room.

Motel Blues

The couple in the bed upstairs
Are really quite a pair
They've been going at it all night long
And clearly just don't care
While as for those in bed next door
They are just the same
I've felt the vibrations through the floor
And it's driving me insane
But they don't care what sleep I've lost
They're simply too engrossed to be
Sympathetic to my frustration
That there is no-one here with me!

My Brother

Could I have done more
In the life we shared?
A more supportive brother?
A closer friend?
Could I have stood by you more than I did?
Annoyed you less
Argued less
Fought less
Now helpless
In your greatest need
Could I have given more of me
In the brief life that we shared?

No Body's Perfect

I like the way you look at me
Your smile really turns me on
Your nose, ears, mouth
They all agree
It's just the rest of you that's wrong!

Not All Wounds Bleed

Disability is not always visible
Violence is not always physical
I may not look like I'm in need
But not everyone's wounds bleed.

Not So Nursery Rhyme – Humpty

Humpty Dumpty sat on a wall
Laughing at all the king's men
He'd been warned before
About the height from the floor
It was an accident just waiting to happen
Then as expected he had the great fall
And landed with a hell of a crunch
So all the king's men
And some of his horses
Had Humpty Dump omelettes for lunch.

Not So Nursery Rhyme – Mary

Mary Mary quite contrary
How does your garden grow?
"Don't be so rude, Im not contrary!
And why the hell do you want to know?"

Not So Nursery Rhyme – Muffet

Little Miss Muffet
Sat on her fat tuffet
Eating her dairy products.
She couldn't sit on a chair
Even if there'd been one there
'Cos her tuffet was overly stuffet.

Not So Nursery Rhyme – Owl

A wise old owl sat in an oak
His eyes as wide as could be
He'd been on social media all day
When he should have been fast asleep
He'd seen and he'd heard so much nonsense
It went against all that he knew
So the wise old owl deleted his accounts
And went back to what owls ought to do.

Not So Nursery Rhyme – Sheep

Baa baa black sheep have you any wool?
"Of course I have, I'm covered in it, I'm a sheep you fool!"

Baa baa black sheep can I have some wool?
I've a jumper to knit to keep me warm, I only want a handful.

Baa baa black sheep it won't take too much time
"Bugger off, it gets cold at night, shear your own skin not mine!"

Not So Nursery Rhyme – York

The grand old Duke of York
He had far too many men
He marched them pointlessly around
Time and time again.

The grand old Duke of York
He marched his men too hard
And when they were only halfway up
They shot the mad bastard.

Pandemic

I can deal with the isolation
And maybe some of the panic
That has kept bad company with me
During the pandemic

But now it looks like it's over
I have a more pressing dilemma
Being face to face with people again
With my broken social antenna.

Parallel Uni-Verse

Just for a moment
Living in
A parallel universe
Watching
Life
Passing by
In my eyes
Images of
Two halves
Separated
My heart

I imagined
A parallel universe
Without you
Friends, living
Without me
A stranger
Estranged
My heart
Universally
Torn apart
Your life

      A parallel universe
           Apart.

Pissing In The Wind

Whichever way you face
Assuming you can choose
Nine times out of ten
You'll end up pissing on your shoes.

Politicians And Prostitutes

The politician by definition
Prostitutes his mind
For party gilded altruism
Another vote to find
The prostitute is more astute
Her manifesto's clear
She plays the game for money
No altruism there.

Pubic Hairs

Have you ever noticed how pubic hairs
Have a wilful life of their own
And apart from the usual bathroom collection
They migrate all over your home.

I've even seen some at the place where I work
Which is always an unpleasant surprise
Their brazen appearance in a public place
Is often difficult to disguise.

But how do they travel, these short curly pubes
Through briefs of tight woven cotton?
It's an enigma to me, but they will always be
An embarrassment to anyone who finds one.

Sheets

Between these sheets
We wrestle
Cheat
Compete
Bend rules
Jostle
Rhythmic
Movement
Indiscrete
Rolling
Sliding
Then replete
We separate
Breathe
New line
New page...

We replicate
In time
We consummate
The perfect rhyme
We guide
To the ultimate
Black on white
We penetrate
Virgin white
We punctuate
All blank space
Between these sheets.

Signal Failure

It is entirely possible
That I
Have misread a signal
Where there were no signs
Read huge volumes of text
Between non-existent lines
Have I
Misunderstood something
That was never really meant?
Imagined a feeling
That you have simply never felt?

Size Is Everything

Some say that size is everything
Actually, I would agree
And for those not quite so fortunate
To be as well-endowed as me
I have few words of comfort
Save for these I now impart
That if your size is compromised
Then do it in the dark!

Speechless

When we met my mouth was dumb
I could not find the words to say
Instead, I tried to use my eyes
Communicate another way
But what lay behind that silent gaze?
What words should you extract?
To help you, help me, penetrate
This verbal cataract?
I fear that what you really saw
Was an unfocused haze
Of prism-fractured meanings
That could be taken several ways
So, you retired gracefully
While teeming I remained
With all the words I meant to say
Frustratingly restrained.

Team Player

Now we can talk in person
I cannot put you on mute
I cannot switch off the video
And walking away is rude
I agree that there are some benefits
But now sitting here in this same place
I object that I have no choice but to listen
To the noise coming out of your face.

The Soul

Where is the soul of modern man?
What organ holds the key?
What assembly of macromolecules
Comprise a personality?
If who I am is what I've learned
Then my soul is in my head
So it's not my heart that holds the key
But my memories instead.

That Kind Of Girl

He was bold
She was naïve
He thought she didn't want to leave
She was not the type to stray
But her innocence got in the way
So
Without the time to think it through
The danger only grew and grew
And
Before she had the time to pause
To say
That's not the kind of girl she was
She was.

The Backside Of Your Smile

Your mouth curled up to greet your eyes
But they did not co-operate
Reluctant to participate
In the exercise
Of perjury
Thus
Abandoned in a sea of ice
Your smiling lips
Frozen
In a bare faced lie.

The Beautiful Chest

There once was a young lady with a beautiful chest
The innuendo, I am sure you'll agree
Caused great consternation to the people she met
When invited to inspect it for free!
Their horrified looks and gasps of surprise
Were a feature of many a conversation
Before they finally understood her innocent intent
And accepted her generous invitation.

It was a fine-looking chest and beautifully smooth
Since she rubbed it with oil once a week
And there were two pretty buttons on top
But, something else made this chest quite unique
You see, the young lady's chest was a magical thing
And if you pressed those two buttons together
Whatever you wished for at that moment in time
Would come true and be yours for ever.

Now one evening the vicar appeared
And without modesty himself professed
That he was rather a well-known expert
On the early 20th century chest
He had heard all the stories of magic
And without listening to words of advice
He would try to press both buttons at once
And make a wish for something nice.

But the vicar, who was advancing in years
Did not have the best use of his eyes

And as he entered the young lady's house
Was in for an unpleasant surprise
As he walked towards the young lady
He tripped, and quite unexpectedly pressed
Two rather fine soft little buttons, but
They were the wrong buttons upon the wrong chest!

The young lady, quite shocked by these pressing advances
Not those you'd expect of the vicar's
Fell backwards and pressed the buttons on the chest
Which she felt through her skirt and her knickers
Suddenly, realizing what she had sat on
In panic stuttered; "I wish, I wish, I wish..."
But the vicar unaware of what she'd done
Cried "Oh shit !" before she could finish.

Suddenly the magic chest, without warning
Or respect for the young lady's stammer
Had filled the whole room and the house where they fell
In the most unpleasant manner!
Now, aside from the mess and embarrassment
And, that a Vicar should always avoid cursing
The moral of this tale is really quite simple
Don't touch any chest without asking.

The Big C

One day we'll crack the code
Solve the mystery
Relegate cancer
To history
In the meantime
Let's put it in its proper place
And always use lowercase.

The Royal Throne

When visiting the royal throne
Does the monarch take a book or mobile phone
To utilize best the time and place
While easing passage of their waste?

Are they usually brisk or slow?
Unsettled by the type of flow?
Does a dietician oversee
To keep their movements trouble free?

When on the throne is the behind
Always properly aligned?
Do they fold or do they scrunch
The toilet paper in a bunch?

And do they ever make a sound
When there is no one else around?
I'd like to think they're a lot like us
Just another job without the fuss.

Thinking About Thinking

The human mind is an astonishing thing
Especially when we start to think about thinking
What is a thought, and where does it begin?
Is it simply a by-product of information we put in?

Our minds are a complex chemical atlas
Of things we have seen, heard, felt, imagined, practiced
So as such an asset, why are we not taught
To think more about thinking and the value of thought?

Remember Rodin's colossal bronze effigy
A poet deep in thought, celebrating mental dexterity
The Thinker (naked but for his thoughts) provides a link
Demonstrating the importance of taking time to think.

Einstein, a man whose mind-modelled experiments
Used thoughts to construct metaphysical evidence
Visions of onrushing trains and mathematics
Establishing concepts in quantum mechanics.

So thinking is a talent, it is not doing nothing
It's exercising our brain to reason about something
So why at school was my reward always lacking
For staring out of the window, when I was thinking... not slacking!

Tongue In Cheek

Oh soft succulent flesh!
Sweet dew-moistened fruit
So arousing and fresh
Although preferably mute
But not without movement
Nor left to run free
Sometimes wasted on words
But never on me!

Travel Tip

In many lands it's commonplace
To use your right hand to feed your face
So, remember what your left hand's for
As you close the toilet door.

Undertakers

Black hats
Black coats
Flat smiles
Black jokes
The undertakers
Undertake
To take you under
Ease your transport
To the other side
Of that metaphysical divide
Behind the scene
Beyond the seam
That separates
Our blue from green
Travel agents
For the tangible
Providing passage to
The unimaginable
Servicing cadavers
For a fee
From the survivors
Undertaking
All we cannot take
And yet, in our wake
Who will undertake
To take them under?
I know
More undertakers!

Valentine

It's that time of year again
When lovers resort to written word
In poems adorned with sappy tripe
Like glitter sparkling on a turd
Drivel much less tolerated
If used at any other time
And "forever" can mean just 12 months
Until the next Valentine.

Lines of verse like tripwires
Trap the unsuspecting amateur
Snaring them in promises
Based on a date in the calendar
So let the inner bard rest in peace
Silence your rhyming couplets
No sappy doggerel please
Just play it safe with chocolates.

Vital Organs

In the garden of Eden, at the dawning of time
God said to man by way of a rhyme
"For you, I have both good news and bad
That is sure to drive Eve and her daughters quite mad"

"Okay" said Adam "First what's the good news?"
God replied "I have new organs for you
One's in your head, let's call it a brain
The other's a penis and will Eve's passion inflame"

"Wow!" said Adam, "That sounds great
But, what was the bad news for me and my mate?"
"The bad news" said God, his expression sublime
"You have only enough blood to use one at a time!"

Warm Seats

Who was it here before me
That felt the need to go?
This almost
Not quite
Touching
Do I really want to know?
If I had only waited
An extra minute in the street
I could have easily avoided
This warm
And very public
Toilet seat.

Wedding Night

A handsome young Italian lost half of his foot
It was an accident back in World War II
But he managed his rehabilitation
Quite well, with a sock stuffed into a shoe.

But late on the night of his wedding
This secret he had failed to disclose
Was going to be rudely discovered
Once he had taken off all of his clothes.

The wife and her husband were upstairs undressing
When a loud scream ripped through the air
The young wife ran to her mother downstairs
"Mamma! his chest it is covered in hair!"

Her mother reassured her that this was quite normal
That she must accept his amorous advances
So the young wife returned to her husband upstairs
Still wondering if she was taking her chances.

Moments later came another loud scream
And the mother raised her eyes in despair
The young wife flew down the stairs to her mum
"Mamma! his legs… they're covered in hair!"

Her mother reassured her this was quite normal
That she should continue to undress the young man
So with slightly more courage than last time

She promised "I will do the best that I can."

The young wife returned to her husband upstairs
With confidence to pursue her intention
To undress and make passionate love to her man
Without any further objection.

But, within minutes she was back down the stairs
And with tears she was wailing again
"But, but... he's only got a foot and a half!"
Her mother replied "Is that any reason to complain!"

When I Lay Down

Is it easier for those that are leaving
Than for those that are left behind?
Is the grief inversely proportional
To your earthly span of time?
Will the hole left in our family
Always be this deep?
Will my pillow always be this damp
When I lay down to sleep?

When Things Go Wrong

When things go wrong
Through no fault of your own
And you get stuck on the wrong side of luck
Just remember
When someone else's shit hits the fan
Shut your mouth and duck!

Wisdom

The lips of a fool are a dangerous tool
Resulting in many a cock-up
The wise know when it's time to speak
And when to shut the fuck up!

Xposure

Now I have exposed myself
For dubious benefit of wealth
In open verse
And printed page
I have laid my soul on a literal stage
But now I can no longer wait
With critics straining at the gate
So let the evil feast begin
Let the Serengeti lions in
Let them pick and chew and gnaw
The very lines I've sought to draw
Food for thought that once was mine
Let them now devour
Line... by... line
Then, as the dust begins to rise
And stifled by their mocking cries
This tattered soul, on which they prey
Will quietly drag himself away.

www.ingramcontent.com/pod-product-compliance
Ingram Content Group UK Ltd.
Pitfield, Milton Keynes, MK11 3LW, UK
UKHW040017070526
12295UKWH00024B/105